I READ! YOU READ!

 Child's Turn to Read

 Adult's Turn to Read

WE READ ABOUT

Self-Esteem

Vicky Bureau and Madison Parker

SEAHORSE PUBLISHING

Parent and Caregiver Guide

Reading aloud with your child has many benefits. It expands vocabulary, sparks discussion, and promotes an emotional bond. Research shows that children who have books read aloud to them have improved language skills, leading to greater school success.

I Read! You Read! books offer a fun and easy way to read with your child. Follow these guidelines.

Before Reading

- Look at the front and back covers. Discuss personal experiences that relate to the topic.
- Read the *Words to Know* at the back of the book. Talk about what the words mean.
- If the book will be challenging or unfamiliar to your child, read it aloud by yourself the first time. Then, invite your child to participate in a second reading.

During Reading

 Have your child read the words beside this symbol. This text has been carefully matched to the reading and grade levels shown on the cover.

 You read the words beside this symbol.

- Stop often to discuss what you are reading and to make sure your child understands.
- If your child struggles with decoding a word, help them sound it out. If it is still a challenge, say the word for your child and have them repeat it after you.
- To find the meaning of a word, look for clues in the surrounding words and pictures.

After Reading

- Praise your child's efforts. Notice how they have grown as a reader.
- Use the *Comprehension Questions* at the back of the book.
- Discuss what your child learned and what they liked or didn't like about the book.

Most importantly, let your child know that reading is fun and worthwhile. Keep reading together as your child's skills and confidence grow.

TABLE OF CONTENTS

Self-Esteem: Do You Have It? 4

Self-Esteem: What Does It Mean? 12

Self-Esteem: How Can You Build Yours? 18

What Would You Do? 20

Words to Know 22

Index 23

Comprehension Questions 23

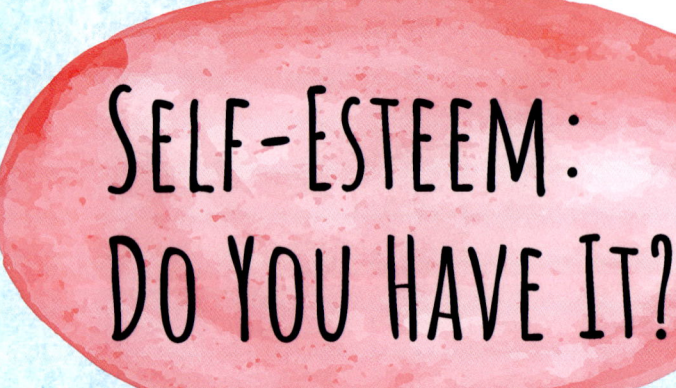

Self-Esteem: Do You Have It?

What is something you're good at? Or proud of?

What do you like most about yourself?

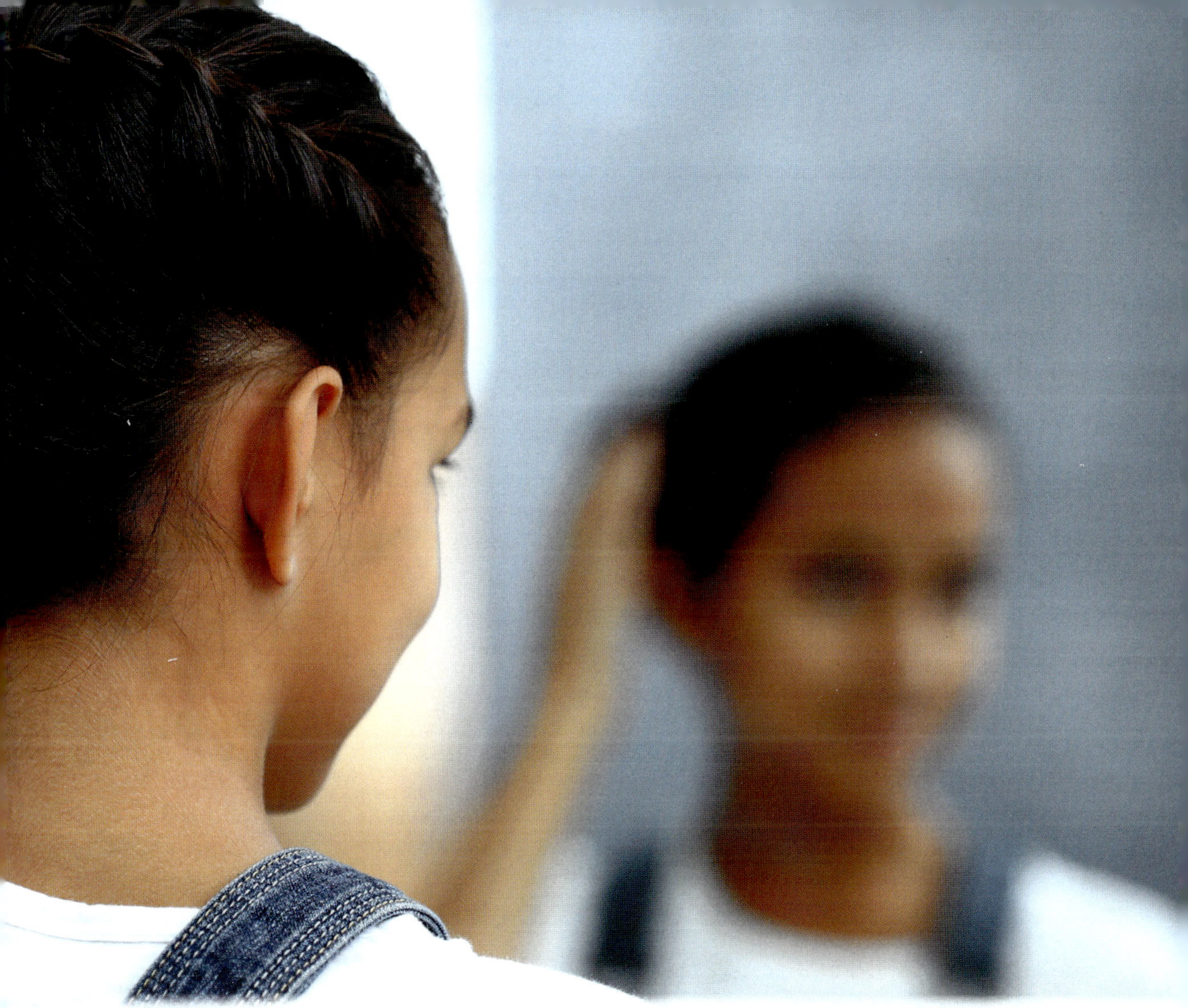

Do you like who you are, or do you sometimes wish you were like someone else?

Sometimes, we want what others have.

Sometimes, we want to do what others do.

We may not understand who we are or **appreciate** what makes us **special**.

ADULT

Self-esteem is like a jar of cookies.

Sometimes, it's full.

Sometimes, you need a refill!

Sometimes, you may feel crumbly.

Sometimes, you may feel sweet!

In other words, look up to others without looking down on yourself.

Admire those around you while also taking **pride** in yourself!

Self-Esteem: What Does It Mean?

What is the best compliment you have ever received? How did it make you feel?

Having **self-esteem** means you feel mostly good about yourself.

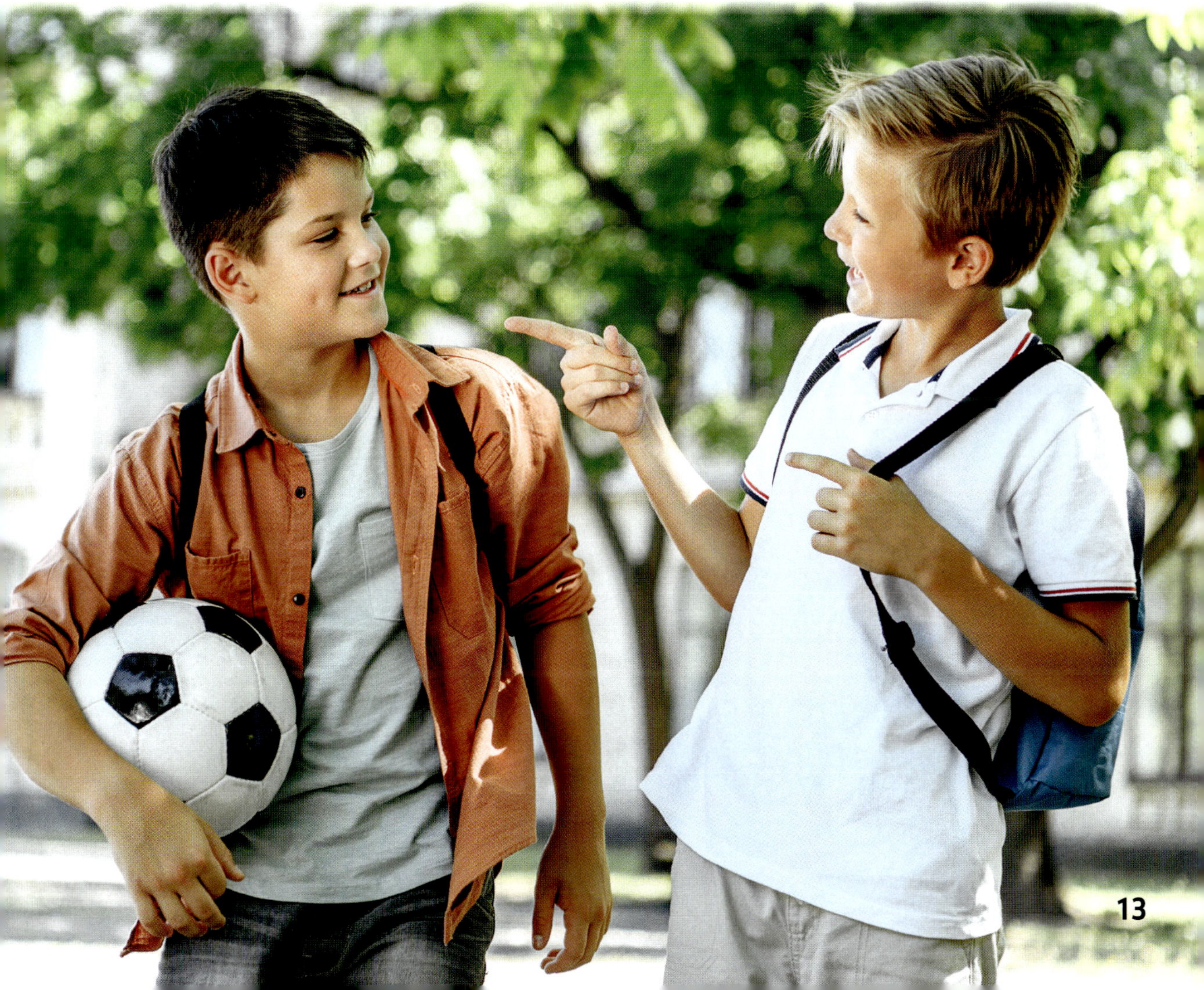

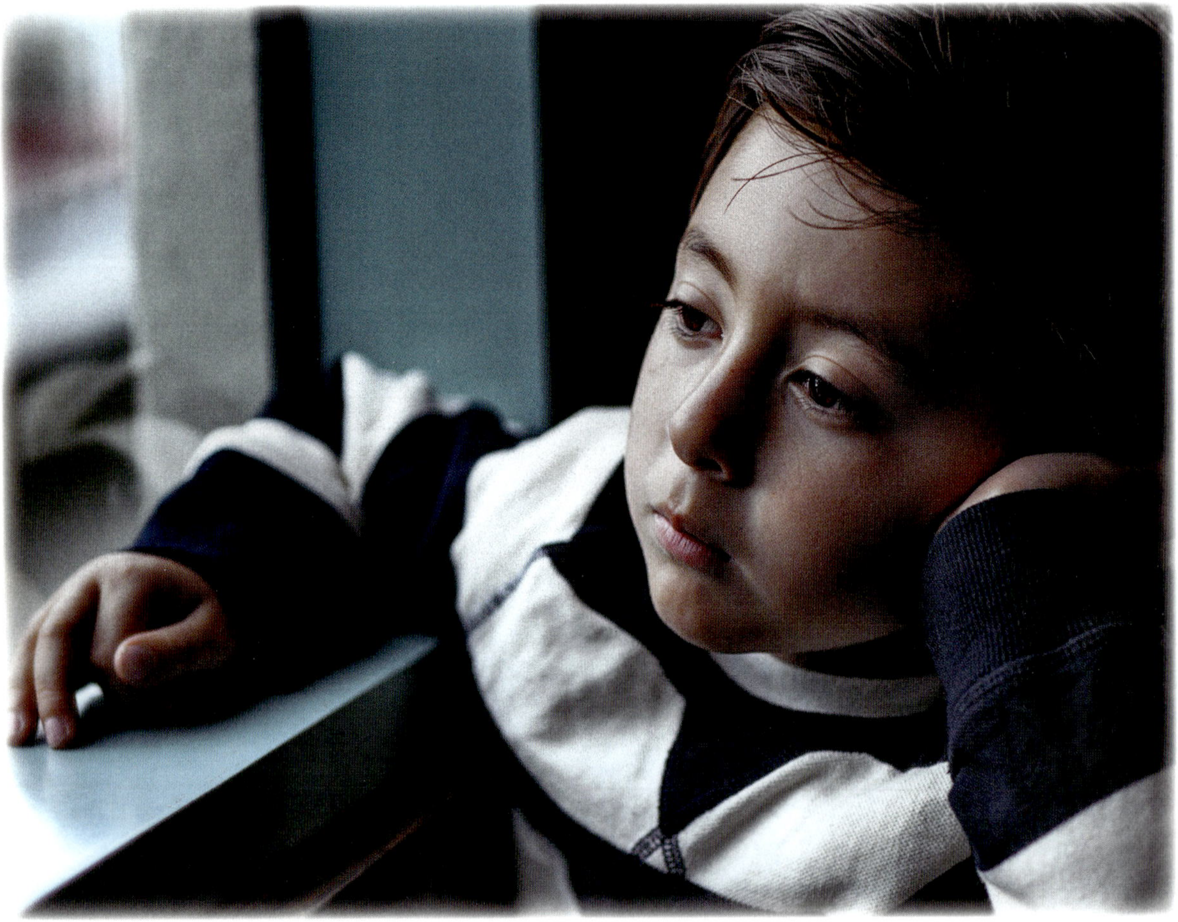

You can't always feel good about yourself.

But feeling mostly good about yourself means that you understand what makes you **unique**, and that you take pride in what you do.

ADULT

Who **inspires** you?

Who helps you feel **special**?

Look within YOU!

ADULT

Self-Esteem: How Can You Build Yours?

You can learn more about yourself! Want to know how?

Ask yourself, "What do I like best about me?" Think less, "I'm different," and more, "I'm unique because of what makes me different!"

What are some things you're good at? CHILD

What are some things you'd like to work on? ADULT

What Would You Do?

Your friend needs help solving a math problem. Do you think you can help?

CHILD

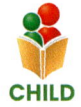

You won a ribbon for your art project. How does it make you feel?

ADULT

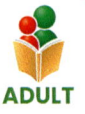

Let's review your answers!

Schoolwork can be challenging. But working hard to find the correct answer helps you build **confidence**!

Being recognized for your accomplishments helps you feel proud of your work and builds self-esteem!

Words to Know

appreciate (UH-pree-shee-ate): to understand the value of something

confidence (KAHN-fuh-dens): a belief that you can succeed

inspires (in-SPIRES): fills someone with an emotion, an idea, or an attitude

pride (prighd): feeling good about what you do

self-esteem (self i-STEEM): feeling happy about who you are

special (SPESH-uhl): different or unusual

unique (yoo-NEEK): being the only one of its kind

Index

admire 11
feel 9, 12, 13, 14, 16, 20, 21
friend 20
good 4, 13, 14, 15, 19

special 7, 16
understand 7, 15

Comprehension Questions

1. How can you show self-esteem even when things seem hard or difficult?

2. What are some things you can do to help build self-esteem?

3. How do the events in someone's life affect their self-esteem?

4. What is the difference between pride and self-esteem?

Written by: Vicky Bureau and Madison Parker
Design by: Under the Oaks Media
Editor: Kim Thompson

Library of Congress PCN Data
We Read About Self-Esteem / Vicky Bureau and Madison Parker
I Read! You Read!
ISBN 979-8-8873-5200-8 (hard cover)
ISBN 979-8-8873-5220-6 (paperback)
ISBN 979-8-8873-5240-4 (EPUB)
ISBN 979-8-8873-5260-2 (eBook)
Library of Congress Control Number: 2022945533

Printed in the United States of America.

Photographs/Shutterstock: Benjavisa Rvangvaree: cover, p. 1; Africa Studio: p. 5; Rob Hainer: p. 6; EvgeniiAnd: p. 7; LimYong Hian: p.8; Oliver Hoffman: p. 9; Robert Kneschke: p. 10; krakenimages: p. 11; Lightfieldstudios: p. 13; Tercer Ojo Photography: p. 14; Robert Kneschke: p. 15; Sergey Novikov: p. 16a; All About Space: p. 16b; Pond Saksit: p. 17a; Irina Kovynyova: p. 17b; Jovica Varga: p. 17c; Motortion Films: p. 19

Seahorse Publishing Company
www.seahorsepub.com

Copyright © 2023 **SEAHORSE PUBLISHING COMPANY**
All rights reserved. No part of this publication may be reproduced, stored in a retrieval system or be transmitted in any form or by any means, electronic, mechanical, photocopying, recording, or otherwise, without the prior written permission of Seahorse Publishing Company.

Published in the United States
Seahorse Publishing
PO Box 771325
Coral Springs, FL 33077

24